NICE

PARTICIPANT'S
GUIDE

Books by Sharon Hodde Miller

Free of Me

Free of Me Participant's Guide

Nice

NICE

PARTICIPANT'S GUIDE

WHY WE LOVE TO
BE LIKED AND HOW
GOD CALLS US TO MORE

Sharon Hodde Miller

BakerBooks

a division of Baker Publishing Group
Grand Rapids, Michigan

Published by Baker Books
a division of Baker Publishing Group
PO Box 6287, Grand Rapids, MI 49516-6287
www.bakerbooks.com

Printed in the United States of America

ISBN 978-1-5409-0014-2

Scripture quotations are from the Holy Bible, New International Version®. NIV®. Copyright © 1973, 1978, 1984, 2011 by Biblica, Inc.™ Used by permission of Zondervan. All rights reserved worldwide. www.zondervan.com. The "NIV" and "New International Version" are trademarks registered in the United States Patent and Trademark Office by Biblica, Inc.™

Portions of this text have been taken from *Nice*, published by Baker Books, 2019.

Author is represented by The Christopher Ferebee Agency, www.christopherferebee.com.

20   21   22   23   24   25   26   7   6   5   4   3   2   1

CONTENTS

INTRODUCTION

"Why are you driving so SLOW!?" I growled at the sluggish car ahead of me. I was already running late to church because I couldn't find one of my children's shoes, and now this driver and every red light seemed to be *conspiring* against me. My blood pressure was rising higher and higher, and I didn't realize how loud my complaint had been until a tiny voice from the back chimed in,

"Mommy, why are you so mad?"

It was a classic case of road rage, and many of us have moments like it. Maybe they are your response to the unrelenting behavior of your kids. Or the rant you posted on social media or the rude comment you made to your spouse. It feels cathartic in the moment, but sometimes it leaves us with regret. "Maybe I should have been a little bit more *nice*."

I'm Sharon Hodde Miller, and I'm so excited to join you in this study of *Nice*. I'm a wife, mom, writer, and more recently, a church planter with my husband, Ike. As a long-time Christ follower, I feel like I've always loved God and the church. But I've noticed something going on in my heart, and in the church, for a while now.

In my first book, *Free of Me*, I describe myself as a "nice Christian girl," and to be honest, it wasn't until recently that I started to see that as problematic.

Niceness. What is this "niceness" all about? Could it perhaps be adding pressure to behave in a certain curated way? Could my little blips of road rage, for instance, be due to that pressure bubbling over? If my quiet, private car is a place where I can comfortably speak unkindly to nearby drivers, perhaps my niceness isn't as fundamental to who I am, or to being a witness to God's love, as I assumed it was. Perhaps it's even causing me to lose sight of the path Jesus wants me to follow.

The truth is that God never called us to be nice. Yet we live in a culture that prizes niceness as one of its highest virtues. Niceness keeps the peace, wins friends, gains influence, and serves our reputations well, but it also takes the teeth out of our witness and the power out of our faith. When we choose to be nice instead of faithful, we bear fruits that are fake, bland, bitter, hard, and rotten to the core. The church is less healthy when all we want is a nice exterior.

The Bible does, however, call us to kindness, gentleness, and love. These fruits of the Spirit come from a healthy "tree" if you will. And as Jesus says, we will know a tree by its fruit.

In this five-session series, we will draw on this tree-and-fruit metaphor to explore the seemingly innocent idol that has crept into our faith and quietly corrupted it, producing several bad fruits. Then we'll challenge each other to cultivate a better "tree," taking practical steps to reclaim our credibility as followers of Christ and bear better, richer, more life-giving fruits.

How to Read the Book as You Watch the Videos

If you are reading *Nice* while you view the videos, please know that they loosely correspond with the following chapters:

Session 1: Chapters 1 through 7
Session 2: Chapters 8 and 9

Session 3: Chapter 10

Session 4: Chapter 11

Session 5: Chapters 12 and 13

The videos do not cover every chapter, which is why you may want to begin by reading the first half of the book, and then pick up the video series when you arrive at chapter 8. No matter the order you choose, it is my prayer that this study will inspire deep conversation and transformative life change as you journey through it!

Lord Jesus, in our pursuit to love like you love, to show the world how wonderful and full of grace you are, we have become a "nice" people—afraid, inauthentic, and shallow. We pray that through this study, you will show us the bad fruits that come from niceness and reveal how we can be your true disciples in a modern world. Lights that shine in the darkness, no matter how intimidating it can be. Amen.

Session 1

The Fruit of Niceness

The temptation of the age is to look good without being good.

Brennan Manning

Niceness is a form of cultural currency. For instance, we are expected to smile at cashiers or speak pleasantries on the phone in order to get all manner of things—from a smooth transaction at the store to a promotion at work. Niceness is a way to get what we want, in small and big ways. Of course, there's nothing wrong with smiling at people (our world could use more civility), but what I am going to address in this series is the ways niceness has evolved beyond social politeness into a transactional crutch.

For many of us, we also use niceness as a way to draw others to Jesus. We think that simply putting a smile on our face will help people see Jesus in us. But is niceness the key to witnessing to Christ's kingdom?

Not when we look at the life of Jesus. Jesus was straightforward and honest, sometimes sad and afraid, sometimes angry, sometimes playful, but he was never simply nice. And this begs an important question. If niceness was never Jesus's public default, why is it ours?

Before watching video 1, read the introduction and chapters 1 through 7 in *Nice*.

1. Did you relate to the story of Sierra or her coworker? Both? Neither?

_____

_____

_____

_____

_____

_____

_____

_____

_____

_____

_____

_____

_____

_____

_____

_____

_____

_____

2. In the first seven chapters of the book, is there anything you read about niceness that you hadn't thought about before?

_____

_____

_____

_____

_____

_____

_____

_____

_____

_____

_____

_____

_____

_____

_____

_____

_____

_____

3. Looking at your own life, in what ways have you used niceness to get things or to have things go your way? Have you used niceness in an attempt to lead people to Jesus? How so?

_____

_____

_____

_____

_____

_____

_____

_____

_____

_____

_____

_____

_____

_____

_____

_____

4. In what ways have you seen niceness take the form of a false virtue in the world? And in what ways have you seen niceness take the form of a false idol in the church?

_____

_____

_____

_____

_____

_____

_____

_____

_____

_____

_____

_____

_____

_____

_____

_____

_____

5. What's the difference between kindness and niceness? Consider Jesus's example. In what ways did Jesus demonstrate this distinction?

_____

_____

_____

_____

_____

_____

_____

_____

_____

_____

_____

_____

_____

_____

_____

_____

_____

_____

6. Consider the Christmas tree example. What does it illustrate about the cost of staying in the nice zone rather than encouraging authenticity?

7. Your spiritual health, or "fruit," matters to those around
you. What does it look like to show others who you are
and whom you follow?

_____

_____

_____

_____

_____

_____

_____

_____

_____

_____

_____

_____

_____

_____

_____

_____

_____

NOTES

_____

_____

_____

_____

_____

_____

_____

_____

_____

_____

_____

_____

_____

_____

_____

_____

_____

_____

_____

_____

_____

NOTES

_____

_____

_____

_____

_____

_____

_____

_____

_____

_____

_____

_____

_____

_____

_____

_____

_____

_____

_____

_____

_____

Session 2

Grow Original

Being noticed is not our food. The approval of others is not our food. . . .
Our food, that which nourishes and makes us whole, is to do God's will.

Marlena Graves

In chapter 9, I wrote about tomatoes and how they vary widely in flavor and texture, depending on how they're grown. Some tomatoes are engineered to look and feel uniform, but this engineering sacrifices the flavor. However, tomatoes from heirloom plants, whose design is original and untouched, are stunningly delicious.

This principle applies to more than just tomatoes. Just about everything tastes better when it's real. Real chocolate tastes much better than the cheap, processed stuff. (Although some would argue the processed stuff is better for s'mores . . . they do have a point.) Real sunshine is much more effective than seasonal affective disorder lights or a vitamin D supplement—as helpful as they can be! Real visits with friends are better than FaceTime sessions.

Fake chocolate, fake sunshine, and digital communication are all *okay*. But they simply pale in comparison to the true forms of authentic goodness. And, of course, you know where I'm going with this—a fake, nice veneer pales in comparison to the true, original, God-given version of ourselves. But how can we find that person when we've been relying on niceness for so long?

Well, we need to prune the fruit and stop the habits that turn us into inauthentic, cheap imitations of ourselves. That's an important start, but Matthew 7 takes us even further, showing us that it's not enough to prune the fruits of our unhealthy trees. Because the fruit is not the problem; instead, it's the result of a much deeper issue. True transformation comes when we cut down the tree.

Before watching video 2, read chapters 8 and 9 in *Nice*.

1. Is there any part of Krista's story that rings true for you? What is it?

_____

_____

_____

_____

_____

_____

_____

_____

_____

_____

_____

_____

_____

_____

_____

_____

_____

_____

_____

2. First Corinthians 3:7 says it's the spirit that provides growth. What does it mean to abide in Christ and how can that help you produce the fruit of the spirit?

_____

_____

_____

_____

_____

_____

_____

_____

_____

_____

_____

_____

_____

_____

_____

_____

3. In John 15:2, Jesus says that God "cuts off every branch in me that bears no fruit, while every branch that does bear fruit he prunes so that it will be even more fruitful." What does it look like for your "tree" to be pruned?

_____

_____

_____

_____

_____

_____

_____

_____

_____

_____

_____

_____

_____

_____

_____

_____

4. Spiritual discipline is one of the ways I believe we can prune our tree. Disciplines like seeing ourselves honestly and the discipline of secrecy. What obstacles to engaging in these spiritual practices do you anticipate dealing with? Have you encountered some already?

_____

_____

_____

_____

_____

_____

_____

_____

_____

What practices have helped you grow? What has _not_ helped you grow?

_____

_____

_____

_____

_____

5. We are often told to be ourselves. What do you think is the difference between the world's version of this message and God's? Consider digging into Scripture for guidance on this.

_____

_____

_____

_____

_____

_____

_____

_____

_____

_____

_____

_____

_____

_____

_____

_____

6. If we are honest with ourselves, most of us are tempted to conform to others' expectations of us more than the desires Jesus has for our lives. How can you see the difference on a daily basis? What should you be looking for, and how can you pivot toward healthy pruning?

_____

_____

_____

_____

_____

_____

_____

_____

_____

_____

_____

_____

_____

_____

_____

_____

NOTES

ᐱᐱᐱᐱ NOTES ᐱᐱᐱᐱ

_____

_____

_____

_____

_____

_____

_____

_____

_____

_____

_____

_____

_____

_____

_____

_____

_____

_____

_____

_____

_____

_____

Session 3

Grow Deep

Hope is not the same as oblivion or naiveté. Hope requires reckoning with the world as it is, with reality.

Karen Swallow Prior

> Deep and wide
> Deep and wide
> There's a fountain flowing deep and wide.

I'm sure many of you remember this song from your childhood. As an adult, I never really gave it much thought, but as I've been writing and thinking about trees and roots, this song has been running through my mind.

In chapter 10, I wrote about how hurricanes can rip up seemingly random trees—some tiny trees remain steadfast while some huge, solid-looking trees fall. But the trees a hurricane rips out are not random; they're actually, in many cases, determined by the depth of their roots. The shallower the roots, the weaker the tree.

I've thought about the concept of shallowness a lot in the context of niceness—about how, when someone is referred to as "shallow," it's almost never a compliment. But isn't that what our niceness can sometimes be? Shallow? And to what benefit? When hurricanes in life come for us, will we stand? Can niceness hold us?

And what about God? The song "Deep and Wide" is so simple but so true about our God. If God were a tree, his roots would run deep *and* wide. Shallowness is most certainly not the way of God, so why is it so often the way of Christians?

Before watching video 3, read chapter 10 in *Nice*.

1. Have you ever gone through a situation similar to what Brooke experienced? What role did your faith play?

_____

_____

_____

_____

_____

_____

_____

_____

_____

_____

_____

_____

_____

_____

_____

_____

_____

_____

_____

2. What are the characteristics of shallow faith?

_____

_____

_____

_____

_____

_____

What do you think kept Brooke in the shallow end of faith?

_____

_____

_____

_____

_____

_____

What has kept you there?

_____

_____

_____

_____

_____

_____

3. On page 156 of *Nice*, I wrote,

> God paints an incredibly layered and complex portrait
> of human nature, so if we are going to believe what God
> says about humanity, we have to hold these seemingly
> opposing truths together. In the one hand we hold our
> boundless brokenness, and in the other we hold our
> identities as image bearers of God. There is not a human
> on the face of the planet for whom both of these state-
> ments is not true, which means our challenge is to up-
> hold them both.

How does knowing this allow us to become spiritually
healthier?

_____

_____

_____

_____

_____

_____

_____

_____

_____

_____

_____

4. In chapter 10, I wrote about Saul's journey to becoming Paul. Once he encountered Jesus, he was forever changed and became a dedicated follower of God. The strength and depth of his faith allowed him to withstand the incredible storms he faced, even with joy. What is the difference between joy and niceness or shallowness?

_____

_____

_____

_____

How can we cultivate joy while still acknowledging harsh truths about people, the world, and ourselves?

_____

_____

_____

_____

I suggest that studying Scripture, worship, and holding on to hope can help us. What else do you believe can help us deepen our roots and move from niceness to true joy?

_____

_____

_____

_____

5. In John 15:5–8, Jesus says,

> I am the vine; you are the branches. If you remain in me
> and I in you, you will bear much fruit; apart from me
> you can do nothing. If you do not remain in me, you
> are like a branch that is thrown away and withers; such
> branches are picked up, thrown into the fire and burned.
> If you remain in me and my words remain in you, ask
> whatever you wish, and it will be done for you. This is
> to my Father's glory, that you bear much fruit, showing
> yourselves to be my disciples.

Thanks be to God that our ability to stand tall in the hurricanes of life is not entirely dependent on our abilities. Our roots are held by God when we anchor them in him. What does it look like to be truly rooted in Christ?

_____

_____

_____

_____

_____

_____

_____

_____

_____

_____

_____

6. We often think of worship as the songs we sing on Sunday. Does that image shift in your mind when it's described as a discipline? If so, how?

NOTES

NOTES

Session 4

Grow Less

We are not what we produce, we are not what we make, we are not what
we do. . . . Our meaning is defined by our Creator.

Ragan Sutterfield

We all know how our culture measures success: achievement, accomplishment, busyness. In contrast to this pace of life, God calls us to rest, but it's a struggle to pursue. Both inside and outside the church, many of us feel the need to do more. Serve more. Witness more. More, more, more. But is more always best?

Part of any healthy tree, as we've learned, is pruning. We can't be healthy if we're overgrown, sapping our resources to their extremes. And it can be jarring to realize that producing fruit doesn't necessarily determine health. Like the peach tree I wrote about in chapter 11, more fruit can sometimes actually damage the tree. It's a case of too much of a good thing.

But niceness can sometimes lead us to do more. Saying no can be incredibly challenging. It stems from the desire to genuinely take care of people, while maintaining our own reputations, which leads us to being stretched too thin.

Sometimes a healthy tree—a healthy Christian—does less, not more.

Before watching video 4, read chapter 11 in *Nice*.

1. "I was trying to be Jesus to everyone," Kayleigh said in the video, "but I didn't know him myself." Have you felt a compulsion to "do more" like Kayleigh? Could that compulsion actually derive from your need to feel liked and accepted? If so, how?

2. Read Ezekiel 3, then consider this quote from scholar Iain Duguid, taken from the *NIV Application Commentary: Ezekiel*, in context.

> What do the models of Jesus and Ezekiel tell us about our efforts in evangelism and missions? In the first place, surely they challenge the common notion in the church that "bigger is always better." There is a lot of pressure from many quarters in our times to measure success in terms of numbers. Whether it is evangelistic crusades that speak of thousands of "decisions for Christ" or popular books that suggest adopting certain methodologies will inevitably bring church growth, the "bigger is better" philosophy reigns in much of the contemporary church.

How does Ezekiel demonstrate this philosophy? Does it illuminate your own path for growing fruits of the spirit?

_____

_____

_____

_____

_____

_____

_____

_____

_____

_____

3. Part of "growing less"—in terms of niceness—is speaking the truth in love. When we are honest with people we love, we risk losing them or upsetting them. But being steadfast is something God calls us to. In Ezekiel 3, God tells Ezekiel to harden his forehead when confronting the Israelites, knowing Ezekiel's mission would fail (in worldly terms).

Why is it wise to harden your forehead (versus your heart), and what might that look like in your life? Have you ever had to confront someone, knowing the confrontation would fail? How did it go and how did it impact your relationship with God?

_____

_____

_____

_____

_____

_____

_____

Have you ever entered a situation *without* hardening your forehead in obedience when you knew you should have?

_____

_____

_____

_____

_____

4. What is the difference between the world's definition of success and God's definition of success?

5. Based on what you have heard and read, which idols, commitments, or priorities do you need to "thin" from your life?

_____

_____

_____

_____

_____

_____

_____

_____

_____

_____

_____

_____

_____

_____

_____

_____

_____

_____

∧∧∧∧∧∧ NOTES ∧∧∧∧∧∧

NOTES

Session 5

Grow Wild

Jesus didn't try to protect people from the wilderness. Instead he led them into it.

Barbara Brown Taylor

"I want to be brave, but I'm scared," my friend Sara's five-year-old son said. We were together with our children at the playground, and her son was trying to gather the courage to slide down an eight-foot pole.

"Bravery isn't bravery if you're not scared, Henry," she replied tenderly. He looked at her with as much understanding as a five-year-old could have, nodded his head, and began to slide down the pole.

I remember looking at Sara for a moment, taking in what she had said. She was and is exactly right. It's not courage if we're not afraid. The presence of fear—the possibility of loss—gives us the opportunity to trust.

I sometimes think that people who could be defined as "wild" are fearless. But is that really true? Perhaps to be wild, to grow wild, is to look into the face of fear and say, "I trust something bigger than my fear. I trust God."

In this final lesson of our journey, through acknowledging our idolatry to niceness, I'd like to take the next step: abandoning the shelter of niceness and meeting Jesus in the wilderness.

Before watching video 5, read chapters 12 and 13 in *Nice*.

1. Maliz's story brings tears to my eyes. Knowing how much the fear of losing her family's love plagued her breaks my heart. It took a major crisis for Maliz to move past the fear that her significance depended on her possessions. How do you think having a sheltered faith contributes to this fear?

_____

_____

_____

_____

_____

_____

_____

_____

_____

_____

_____

_____

_____

_____

_____

2. Like hothouse tomatoes, a secure and sheltered faith is bland and ineffectual. We are called to go out into the world and face hardships, even though it's scary. How can the story of Esther teach us to cultivate courage in the face of such dangers? What dangers do you face now that make you want to remain sheltered?

_____

_____

_____

_____

_____

_____

_____

_____

_____

_____

_____

_____

_____

_____

_____

3. Like Esther, who could have retreated into the privilege of the palace, we are tempted to use niceness to shelter ourselves. However, the story of Esther reminds us that sometimes we must expose ourselves to risk and place "a higher good above a lower good." In chapter 12, I talked about disciplines that can help with this call. Which of these disciplines is of highest priority for you?

_____

_____

_____

_____

_____

_____

_____

_____

_____

_____

_____

_____

_____

_____

_____

4. Has this journey of distinguishing niceness from true discipleship to Christ been helpful to you? If so, how?

_____

_____

_____

_____

_____

_____

_____

Write down any specific steps you are planning to take to cultivate a healthier, deeper faith, even if that means "doing less."

_____

_____

_____

_____

_____

_____

_____

NOTES

NOTES

Sharon Hodde Miller leads Bright City Church in Durham, North Carolina, with her husband, Ike. In addition to speaking all over the country and earning her PhD, she is the author of *Free of Me: Why Life Is Better When It's Not about You*. Sharon has been a regular contributor to sites like She Reads Truth, Propel, and *Christianity Today*, and she has blogged at SheWorships.com for over ten years. When she is not leading, teaching, or writing, her favorite place to be is at home with her husband and three kids.

Connect with
Sharon!

To learn more about Sharon's
writing and speaking, visit

SheWorships.com

f SharonHoddeMiller

🐦 SHoddeMiller

📷 SharonHMiller

Turn Your Focus from
Self to Savior

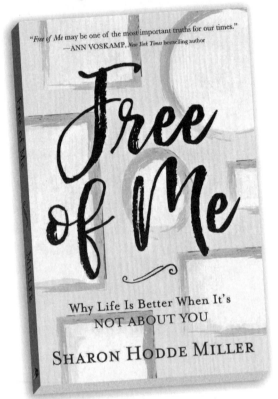

"Free of Me may be one of the most important truths for our times."
—ANN VOSKAMP, *New York Times* bestselling author

Free of Me

Why Life Is Better When It's
NOT ABOUT YOU

SHARON HODDE MILLER

"In a culture captivated by self, this book is a must-read."

—CHRISTINE CAINE, founder of A21 and Propel Women

Experience the

Full Curriculum

BakerBooks
a division of Baker Publishing Group
www.BakerBooks.com

Available wherever books and ebooks are sold.

God Doesn't Call Us to
SUCCEED.
He Calls Us to OBEY.

When we choose to be nice instead of faithful, we bear fruits that are bland, bitter, empty, or rotten to the core. Reclaim your credibility as followers of Christ and bear better, richer, more life-giving fruits.

Experience the
FULL CURRICULUM